The Dogecoin Standard

The Case for Dogecoin and Against Fiat Currencies

Sebastian Walden

Copyright © 2021 Sebastian Walden

All rights reserved

ISBN: 9798733724034

No part of this book may be reproduced, or stored in a retrieval system, or transmitted in any form or by any means, electronic, mechanical, photocopying, recording, or otherwise, without express written permission of the publisher.

Dedicated to all Shiba Inus worldwide.

Contents

INTRODUCTION..1

A BRIEF HISTORY OF MONEY.......................5

BASIC ECONOMIC PRINCIPLES..................19

THE BOOM AND BUST CYCLE....................29

THE FAILURE OF FIAT CURRENCIES.........38

Cryptocurrencies...48

THE CASE FOR DOGECOIN.........................60

REFERENCES...75

INTRODUCTION

Imagine a place called Dogeville. There many doges produce and exchange diverse products and services in the market. The main problem of this city-state is that there is no such thing as money, so the doges recur to barter to fulfill their needs. This causes many unnecessary complications, since every time a doge wishes to acquire a good, he must find another doge that offers such good and that is also willing to accept what he has to offer in return. Other obstacles faced are the impossibility of subdivision of goods and the lack of a standard unit of account. If a doge wants to exchange a cow for wheat, he must accept more wheat than he can store just for the exchange to be fair. The barter system in Dogeville is very inefficient, limits economic growth, and causes the doges many headaches.

The main characteristic of a good currency is not its portability or its divisibility, but its trustworthiness. The agents involved in an economic transaction will only accept payment in a kind of money they know others will accept for a roughly equivalent value of goods. Since doges are not naive, they won't blindly place their trust in any commodity to serve as money; they need something that meets some very specific requirements.

The first requirement any good money must

meet is scarcity; as nothing is valuable unless it is available in a limited quantity. Rare items like diamonds or precious metals are very valuable. The opposite happens with extremely abundant items that no one is willing to pay for, like sand in a beach. Following the law of supply and demand, if the supplied quantity of a commodity grows relative to the demand, its price diminishes. The same happens with money, as it loses its purchasing power with inflation.

The second requirement desirable in a good and trustworthy currency is decentralization. As Lord Acton said: "Power corrupts, and absolute power corrupts absolutely." For argument's sake, let's suppose that Dogeville's dwellers decide to act naively and use gold as a currency, but give the central government the monopoly over minting coins. This may work well for a while, as the officially issued currency is recognizable and uniform, facilitating exchanges. Eventually, a populist and short-minded governor is elected to power and recognizes an opportunity to increase his popularity taking advantage of the monopoly he has over minting. An increase in government spending would temporarily boost the economy, benefitting his image, but if he has to pay for it with taxes it wouldn't be a popular measure. The governor realizes that he can pay for his proposals debasing the currency; this means, combining the gold with a cheaper metal so that he can mint more coins, but conserving their previous nominal value. A coin that previously contained one ounce of gold would now contain 90% of it but would have to be accepted in exchanges as if it had the same value as before. This causes the money supply to increase and its value to diminish. Part of the purchasing power that belonged to the doges has been transferred to the government as a form of indirect taxation, without them being able to do anything about it. If the governor decides to abuse this power, debasing the currency even more, the trust that was placed upon it would gradually be lost, resulting in hyperinflation. The same danger would have existed if the designated medium of exchange would have been a fiat currency, such as the dollar or euro.

Let's reimagine the previously described situation but with a decentralized currency. The gold would be minted into coins in several decentralized mints that had gained the confidence of their clients over time. Doges with gold ingots would go to mints with recognized and trusted brands that minted coins with the amount of gold they claimed to be worth. If a particular mint decides to debase the coins they minted to increase their profits, the public would soon find out and coins produced there would stop being accepted.

Characteristics such as portability, divisibility, durability, transferability, uniformity, and acceptability are also essential for any good currency, but the two previously explained are the ones that have more impact on its trustworthiness. Money that is not highly divisible may make small transactions more difficult, but money whose issuance is centralized in an untrustworthy and highly inflationist government will be almost worthless. The doges must certainly take the previous considerations into account when selecting their currency.

This book is an attempt to explain some basic economic principles in the most rigorous, yet understandable way possible, and to use these principles to make the case for the adoption of the Dogecoin Standard. Furthermore, it is an inquiry into currencies, their history, characteristics, and relation with economic wellbeing. At the end of this book, the argument against fiat currencies and why they can be damaging to the economy will be thoroughly explained; and the case for cryptocurrencies, and more specifically Dogecoin, to serve as commonly used currencies will be made.

A BRIEF HISTORY OF MONEY

Throughout history, money has taken many different shapes and forms, but the functions it has served have been the same: a medium of exchange, a unit of account, and a store of value. It can be defined as anything that is commonly accepted within a society in exchange for goods and services.

Before money was invented, people had to resort to barter. This is the direct exchange of goods and services for other goods and services without the intermediation of money. It is highly inefficient because of the need for a double coincidence of wants, the lack of a standard unit of value, and the indivisibility or perishability of certain goods.

One of the oldest forms of money was cattle. After cows first were domesticated, around 9.000 B.C., they began being used as a medium of exchange[1]. Other animals, like goats and camels, were also used as money. Even today, cattle are used as money in certain parts of Africa. Other commodities, like salt and animal skins, have also been used as money.

Around 1.200 B.C. cowrie shells began being used as money in China[2]. These shells have also been used as a payment method in North America, Africa,

Asia, and Oceania, and their use continued in certain parts of the world until the 19th century. The first use of a metallic object as money is registered in China[3] around the year 1.000 B.C. These coins took the form of imitations of cowrie shells. Similar coins started being used in India several hundred years later.

The first officially minted coins were made in the kingdom on Lydia, under the rule of King Alyattes[3]. They were made of gold, silver, bronze, and other metals; and were stamped with an image on one of its sides, commonly the head of the king. These coins rapidly spread through Greece and Italy around the year 500 B.C.

The use of a hard currency was soon picked up by governments because it facilitated economic transactions and the collection of taxes. The first Roman coins were minted in Neapolis[4] in 326 B.C. In 211 B.C the silver denarius was introduced into the Roman Republic. The quinarius was also intruded which was worth half a denarius, and the sestertius, which was worth half a quinarius. By the first century, B.C Roman coins were uses across the Mediterranean. With the rise of the Roman Empire, Julius Caesar issued coins with his image, to serve also as a medium of propaganda[4].

As taxation not always met all of the imperial budgets, several emperors decided to debase the currency to supply the remaining funds. In the year 64 A.D. Nero reduced the gold content in coins by 4.5%

and silver content by 11%, maintaining their face value intact. By the time Marcus Aurelius was emperor the denarius only contained 75% silver. Commodus, Septimus Severus, and Caracalla kept debasing the currency until the denarius contained less than 1% silver by the year 265 A.D[4]. Following Gresham's law, the older coins with more silver content were hoarded or melted and disappeared from circulation, while the debased coins were used for paying taxes and other daily transactions. As the supply of coins had risen dramatically and their silver content diminished, hyperinflation followed, crippling the economy. To stop the inflationary cycle, Emperor Diocletian imposed price controls in 301 A.D., but this only led consumers to the black market. He also created a new coin called the argenteus, which was worth 50 denarii, but this was only a cosmetic fix and could not restore the trust in the currency[5]. For the following years, inflation continued and mutinies arose when the government was unable to pay the troops. The emperors raised taxes, but economic disparity grew, being the poor the most affected. In the year 476 A.D., following a prolonged economic crisis and military defeats against invading Germanic tribes, the Roman Empire fell.

Silver denarius 44 BC

Silver denarius 274 AD

I contain 95% silver and am the official currency of the most powerful empire in the world.

I contain less than 5% silver and am the official currency of a failing empire burdened in an economic crisis.

Figure 1. Silver denarius

The first use of paper money ever recorded was in China in the 11th century A.D[6]. Because of the inconvenience of carrying heavy strings of coins around, merchants began leaving them with a trustworthy private keeper. In return, they received a paper note indicating how much money they had deposited. These pieces of paper could be traded for goods or be redeemed for the coins stored. During the early years of the Song Dynasty, the government gave licenses to certain certified deposit shops where people could leave their coins in exchange for promissory notes. In the 12th century, the authorities decided to take control of these deposit shops, and thus, the first government-issued paper money was born[6]. The

Chinese government created several money-printing factories in different locations across the country, using special fibers in their paper to prevent counterfeiting. These notes could only be used in particular regions of the empire. In the year 1265 the first national currency was issued, which was backed by gold and silver[6].

The Mongol invasion of China by Kublai Khan gave rise to the Yuan Dynasty in the year 1271. This dynasty issued the Chao, its own form of paper currency, that was initially backed by silver[6]. The biggest problem the Chinese faced with money was that it was too easy to create. As a consequence of this, too much money was issued and it dropped in value, leading to hyperinflation. The Yuan dynasty collapsed in the year 1368 with a highly devaluated currency. The ensuing Ming Dynasty continued printing unbacked fiat money but halted its actions around the year 1450 when the Chao had become virtually worthless[6]. Government-issued paper money was not used again in China until the end of the 19th century when the Qing Dynasty began printing yuan banknotes.

During the Middle Ages, gold, silver, and other metals were used as money. Coins were minted by the rulers in state mints and had the face of the ruler printed on them. On occasions, kings debased the currency to finance wars or to repay debts, which led to inflation, rising prices, and a loss in the purchasing power of money. Princes charged a tax on coinage, called the seigniorage, so they took a profit every time a merchant took bullion to the mint for it to be turned into coins. To incentivize the merchants to take the precious metals to their mints rather than to foreign mints, they offered to return more coins (debased) for a smaller amount of silver. As inflation is not an immediate phenomenon, this practice generated princes and merchant earnings at the expense of the common people, for they could purchase goods at the previous price level with the new money. The opposite of debasement is renforcement, which consists of restoring the amount of precious metal to its original value in a previously debased coin. This was undertaken several times to counter the effects of inflation, but in the long run, there were more debasements than renforcements, so there was a progressive diminution in the purchasing power of money, to the benefit of the rulers[7].

With the discovery and posterior conquest of the New World by Spain, there was a large influx of gold and silver into Europe. The rise in the amount of money led to a decrease in its value because too much money chased too few goods. Despite the large quantities of gold and silver that were carried in galleons from the New Continent, the Spanish economy stagnated relative to other European economies. Over the next century and a half, prices rose sixfold, until inflation finally stabilized when the volume of precious metals imported diminished[8].

The first official form of paper money in Europe

was issued in Sweden in the year 1661. Given the controversy surrounding this event, the monetary authorities certified the banknotes with the signature, by hand, of more than 16 trustworthy officials[9]. The government also guaranteed that all banknotes could be redeemed in species at any time. As pieces of paper were easier to carry and exchange than large and heavy tokens of gold and silver, the banknotes soon became a success, and the system was imitated by other countries across Europe. Not all European bankers had the rigor of the swedes, and they soon realized that not all banknotes circulating would be redeemed. This opened the opportunity for governments to begin issuing banknotes that exceeded their reserves of gold and silver. Whenever more money was needed, the printing press just issued another batch. This had two chief consequences: inflation and economic instability. Whenever there was a panic, banks had a high risk of going bankrupt, as people ran to them to redeem their banknotes in gold. Because of the lack of laws regarding money printing, cities, banks, and institutions saw the opportunity to make a profit and began issuing their own banknotes. Their value was determined by the reputation of the issuer and the backing in species it had. Some of these private entities followed the same unsound monetary practices as governments, which caused their banknotes to trade at a discount or to not be accepted at all.

In 1844, Sir Robert Peel, the prime minister of Great Britain decided to reform the English banking system inspired by the ideas of the Currency School. These economists analyzed fractional reserved banking and showed how the artificial expansion of banknotes and credit by the banks created a boom in the business cycle, which later was followed by inflation and an economic contraction. According to them, the unsound money practices were responsible for the boom-and-bust cycle. Peel introduced the Bank Charter Act, which gave the Bank of England the monopoly over issuing banknotes. It also established that all banknotes issued by this bank had to be backed 100 percent by gold or silver. This act was ultimately a failure and did not eliminate business cycles, since it made the mistake of not considering demand deposits as part of the money supply and overlooked their inflationary potential[10].

In the United States, during the Revolutionary War, the Continental Congress and the colonies issued a form of paper money called continentals to help pay for the war efforts. This currency was not backed by any asset, and Congress issued enormous amounts of it, which caused its purchasing power to plummet. After the Thirteen Colonies gained their independence, the government addressed this issue by passing the Coinage Act of 1792. This resolution gave Congress the sole authority to mint money and established the penalty of death for the debasement of coins by the officers of the mint[11].

With the outbreak of the Civil War in 1861, both the Union and the Confederate states were forced to look for resources to finance the conflict. The South printed a huge amount of treasury notes, which produced annual inflation of 140% from 1961 to 1963[12]. To finance the war effort of the Union, Congress authorized the U.S. Treasury to issue paper money for the first time in the form of non-interest-bearing notes. This also generated inflation, but as the North was richer and had fewer expenses remaining to pay, the total inflation from 1861 to 1865 was 117%. When the war ended, the cost of living in the South was 92 times what it was before the war started[12].

Following the end of the Civil War, the United States remained in the gold standard. This produced some instability, as gold prices dropped every time large gold deposits were found. In 1913 the Federal Reserve was created to stabilize the currency and to regulate banking. Its main functions were conducting the monetary policy, regulating banks, stabilizing the economy, and providing funds to the Federal Government and private banks[13]. The Federal Reserve is allowed to make loans to banks; which can be used as a lender of last resort when private banks face liquidity problems or to manipulate the economy via expansive or contractive policies. The rate at which the Fed lends money to commercial banks is called the discount rate and has great influence over the money supply, inflation, and interest rates. The Fed is also in charge of issuing the entire supply of paper money.

Although the Federal Reserve notes issued by

the Fed were convertible to gold, this didn't mean that the United States was on the gold standard. The price of gold was manipulated by the government, so technically the country operated on a fiat money regime14. The main objective of the creation of the Fed was not to replace the gold standard but to eliminate panics and instability created by the fluctuating price of gold. After the creation of the Fed, the price of gold in the United States was not in accordance with international prices but was set through a commodity-price stabilization scheme. This way, bullion was bought and sold at a fixed price, not necessarily reflecting what the real price would be in a free market. As explained by economist Robert Hetzel[14], the price level was not inversely related to the commodity value of gold.

The Federal Reserve was forced by law to keep enough gold reserves to cover their notes. During the first World War, there was a great influx of gold from Europe to America. To offset the loss of gold, Great Britain inflated her money supply, trying to return to the gold exchange rate that was held before the war. In the United States during the 1920s the economy kept growing rapidly with easy access to credit. In 1923 the Fed even increased the discount rate as they believed economic recovery was too fast. In 1925 the governor of the New York Federal Reserve Bank, Benjamin Strong, proposed a policy that would devalue the dollar to aid the British in their attempt to reverse the money flow. This was achieved by the Federal Reserve lowering the discount rate and making massive security purchases[15]. As a result of this, the gold stock fell from $4.3 billion in 1927 to $3.8 billion in 1928[16]. The gold flow reversed from America to Europe, which allowed Great Britain and France to stay on the gold standard with their devalued currencies. In the U.S economy, the increase in the money supply led to rising prices and a speculative bubble in the stock market. The Wall Street crash of 1929 led to the start of the Great Depression.

In 1931 Great Britain became the first country to drop off the gold standard, and other countries soon followed, as it limited their capacity to increase the money supply. In the United States, people began hoarding gold because of their lack of trust in the banks. The Fed kept raising interest rates to make the dollar more valuable and stop people from converting their dollars into gold so that reserves were not depleted. This made many companies go bankrupt and drastically increased unemployment. Presidents Hoover responded to the economic recession with massive government intervention[15]. He encouraged to continue employing workers without wage cuts and persuaded banks to lend money to other failing banks. In 1930 congress passed a tariff act increasing taxes on imported goods, trying to encourage the production of domestic goods. This was met by retaliatory tariffs, which ultimately only served to worsen the ongoing depression. The Hoover administration also passed several bills providing incentives for several industries and creating public works to increase employment.

None of these policies were very successful and unemployment reached 25% towards the end of Hoover's term. In 1933 Franklin D. Roosevelt became president and expanded even more Hoover's programs. That same year he signed an executive order that prohibited the hoarding of gold. Banks, businesses, and individuals had to sell all their gold for a fixed price set by the government. In 1934 Congress passed the Gold Reserve Act, which transferred all gold reserves to the U. S. Treasury at a discount, converting gold from a currency into a commodity[17]. This law allowed the government to increase the money supply by devaluating the dollar. The U. S. economy slowly began growing, but it did not recover completely until after the Second World War. Economist Murray Rothbard argues that the Keynesian economic policies adopted by Hoover and Roosevelt didn't solve the crisis, but expanded it. By doing this, the government redirected the labor and capital away from their most productive uses to those that were favored by bureaucrats[15]. The devaluation of the dollar was a tax on all money holders and it increased uncertainty even more.

During the later years of the Second World War, there was a need for an efficient foreign exchange system to prevent money devaluation and promote economic growth[18]. With these ends in mind, in 1944, delegates from 44 countries met in Bretton Woods, New Hampshire at the United Nations Monetary and Financial Conference. Thus, the Bretton Woods Agreement was signed, and a new international currency exchange regime was created. Under this system, international currencies were pegged to the U.S dollar, and the dollar was pegged to gold. This helped promote international trade and provided it with stability.

The Bretton Woods Agreement came to an end in 1971, under the government of Richard Nixon. Because the gold reserves were exceeded by the dollars in circulation, Nixon devalued the dollar relative to gold, and after a run on the reserves, he temporarily suspended the U.S. dollar's convertibility into gold[19]. This suspension became permanent in 1973 when the last link between the dollar and gold was severed. Countries could now peg their currencies to a foreign currency, as many countries did with the dollar, or just let its value float freely. In 1974 president Ford signed a bill that allowed to freely trade of gold as a commodity. From 1974 to 1980 the price of gold rose by 385% as more people sought it as a way to protect themselves against inflation[19].

The main benefit of a 100% gold-backed dollar is that it imposed economic discipline to the government. The amount of new money that could be issued was limited by the existing gold reserves. With an unbacked dollar, this limitation doesn't exist. Theoretically, the government could print as much new dollars as they wanted without any constraint. The U.S dollar remains valuable solely because of the faith people have in the government, but there has been a significant lack of discipline in government spending, which has caused rising inflation and massive federal debt, exceeding $28 trillion by January 2021. The expansive monetary policies and market manipulation by governments have led to several recessions, being the 2008 financial crisis the most notable in recent history.

Governments' answer to this crisis was bailing out big banks, pumping more money into the economy, and lowering interest rates, the same actions that led to the creation of the market bubble in the first place. Proponents of modern monetary theory proclaim that governments that issue their own fiat currency can spend as much money as they want, regardless of tax income, covering the deficit by printing more money. These reckless monetary policies will likely lead to a more severe financial crisis in the future.

Because of the lack of faith in the current financial system, in 2008 Satoshi Nakamoto created Bitcoin, the first cryptocurrency. This form of money is decentralized and therefore does not require trust in the government. It also allows for transactions at very low fees without the need for an intermediary. Since then, many more cryptocurrencies and tokens have been created, being Ethereum, Litecoin, Cardano and Ripple the more popular of them. In 2013, software engineers Billy Markus and Jackson Palmer created Dogecoin, a cryptocurrency that is fun, friendly, and free from government manipulation.

BASIC ECONOMIC PRINCIPLES

The objective of this chapter is to explain three basic economic principles that will be very useful to answer the following three questions:

1. What makes Dogecoin valuable?

2. Why are fiat currencies unreliable?

3. Why Dogecoin could be a better form of money than fiat currencies?

The concepts of value, interest and money are introduced here, and will be used to fully answer the previous questions in the following chapters.

Value

What is it precisely that determines the value of something? Is it its scarcity, production cost, some intrinsic quality, or labor requirement? Economists over time have been trying to answer this question with many different theories.

Adam Smith suggested in his magnum opus "The Wealth of Nations" that value is an intrinsic characteristic, or that it belongs to a good for its own sake. Smith proposed the labor theory of value, which claims that the economic value of a good depends on the work necessary to produce it. A chair, then, would be valuable because a lumberjack had to cut down a tree to get the wood, and then a carpenter had to spend time and effort making the chair. Karl Marx used the labor theory of value as a foundation for his theory of surplus-value, which explained that as all value was created by labor, and the proletariat was doing all the manual labor, the capitalist was stealing from the value created by the laborers work to make a profit.

Smith's idea was further developed by David Riccardo and Frederic Bastiat, who proposed the cost theory of value. According to this theory, the value of something is the cost of the labor and resources that went to produce it. This theory can be illustrated by a shirt that needs $4.5 worth of labor and $5 of fabric for its production. This shirt would be worth $10 considering a 5% return on investment. If the market price drops, producers would stop making shirts, but if it rises the growth in ROI would encourage more producers to make shirts, which in the long term would reduce the rate of profit to the market average. The main fault of this theory, as economist Robert P. Murphy[20] points out, is that it doesn't explain the determinant of market prices, just the relation among market prices. The cost of the fabric needed to make the shirt is also a price. If this price were to rise, the cost theory of value could explain the mechanisms by which it would be restored to its "natural price", but is unable to explain what caused the initial variation of this price. If a company decides to spend double the resources making a standard good, they would be unable to charge double the market price for that good. Just because has a certain production cost doesn't mean people will pay for it.

Carl Menger, the father of Austrian economics, refuted this train of thought when he proposed the subjective theory of value, claiming that the value of a good is not something inherent, but it depends on the importance each acting individual places on it as a means to the satisfaction of his needs[21]. The subjective valuation a person makes of a good is not always rational in the homo œconomicus sense of the word. This valuation takes emotional, psychological, and economical factors into account and can vary with time and circumstances. A person could be willing to pay more for a bottle of water when he is thirsty than when he is fully hydrated. Likewise, a winter coat is more valuable for someone that lives in a cold place than for someone that lives in the tropics.

The means people have to satisfy their ends are scarce, and therefore the ends more highly valued will be fulfilled and the least important will not[21]. The subjective theory of value does not assume that people assign cardinal units of value to goods, but they can be ranked from most preferred to least preferred. A person at a certain moment can prefer eating ice cream to a piece of cake, without ever assigning x units of happiness to the ice cream and y units of happiness to the cake. Goods in the scale of value can be ranked with ordinal numbers, not cardinal. Therefore, value can only be ranked, not measured, and varies from person to person. Menger also introduced marginal analysis to his theory of value. A thirsty person would place a higher value in the first glass of water he drinks, that would quench his thirst, than on the second or third one, whose marginal utility would be much lower.

According to Menger, an exchange occurs when a person gives something he values less in exchange for something he values more. In any voluntary transaction both involved parties win, insomuch as otherwise there would be no transaction at all, as no one would give a good he values more for one he values less. In a market transaction, the seller of a good will only accept an amount of money he values more than the good he has, and a buyer will only pay for something if he deems it preferable to the money he has in hand. If there is no common ground between these two prices, no exchange will occur. Market prices are usually set by the consensus of the subjective valuation of buyers and sellers.

Applying the subjective value theory to the case in study, it results evident that currencies are not valuable because of any intrinsic property, but solely because people deem them valuable. Even currencies backed by gold and silver have no intrinsic value. The value of any currency, including cryptocurrencies, is determined by the subjective valuation of people. This valuation is often influenced by the usefulness of the currencies, as people value highly those things that help them fulfill their needs. Since any economy needs a reliable store of wealth and a convenient medium of exchange, those currencies that help fulfill these needs will be regarded as valuable and those that do not will not be worth much.

Interest

Interest can be broadly defined as the cost of using somebody else's money. This definition raises the question: What determines the rate an investor is willing to accept for his savings? To answer this question, economist Eugen von Bohm-Bawerk developed the Time preference Theory of Interest.

All people, under equality of circumstances, prefer to attain their ends sooner rather than later, or in economic terms, prefer present consumption over future consumption. This is known as the law of time preference. This preference can be felt with different intensity by each person in different moments. An opportunity for an exchange arises when a person with a high time preference meets a person with a low time preference. Those who resign to present goods in exchange for a higher quantity of future goods are lenders, and those who resign to future goods for a lesser amount of goods in the present are called borrowers. The ratio at which people exchange goods in the present for goods in the future in the time market is called the interest rate[22].

According to economist Jesus Huerta de Soto[23], the loan market is just a small portion of the whole money market in which goods and services are exchanged for monetary units and in which prices are determined. Even if loans didn't exist in an economy, there would still be an interest rate as economic agents would invest their savings directly exchanging present for future goods.

In a society with low time preference, there would be a lot of savings, and therefore the interest rate would be low, as a lot of people would be willing to renounce present consumption in exchange for more consumption in the future. In a society with a very high time preference, savings would be small and the interest rate would be high, as more people would be willing to renounce to consumption in the future in exchange for more consumption in the present.

Entrepreneurs always want to make profits. To achieve this end, they invest either their own savings or the savings of other people they have borrowed in the projects that have a higher yield than the market interest rate. If an investment opportunity has a lower expected return than the market interest rate, it will be more profitable to lend the money than to invest it directly. In a society with a high interest rate, savings available for investment are very low, so only the more profitable ventures can be undertaken. If there are a lot of savings available, the interest rate will be low, and entrepreneurs will invest even in some businesses with medium expected profitability. This would be the ideal configuration under an unregulated interest rate, but on occasions governments, through central banks, manipulate interest rates trying to generate economic growth. Whenever the GDP is not growing as expected, central bankers have been known to artificially lower the interest rate through monetary policies. Entrepreneurs take notice of the low-interest rates and invest in those businesses that have a higher expected return than the new manipulated interest rate. Many of these investments are made in projects that wouldn't normally be profitable, but appear profitable because of the artificially low interest rate. The result of this interest rate manipulation is a malinvestment of society's scarce savings, as resources are used in a way that does not reflect the real wants of society. Misallocation of resources inevitably leads to a waste of capital and the need for an economic readjustment.

Money

Money is an economic good that is generally used as a medium of exchange. According to economist Carl

Menger[23], money emerged in a non-intentional way as many people were looking to satisfy their need to conduct exchanges in the easiest way possible. The precursor to money, barter, is very primitive and is limited to situations in which there exists a double coincidence of wants. Money makes transactions easier and more efficient, and consequently increases the number of exchanges made and helps to the development of society. The more acceptance a form of money has, the more useful it is. Money, as a medium of exchange, is also an economic good, and must therefore be scarce to have value. The amount of money is not as important as the changes in its quantity. The amount of goods people are willing to give for a certain sum of money is its purchasing power[23].

The price of money is determined by its supply and demand. An increase in the supply of money will tend to lower its purchasing power. If a government decreed that all monetary units of its currency would now be worth two monetary units, prices would be immediately adjusted and nothing would change. In this situation, the alteration would be merely nominal, but this hypothetical case varies significantly from the real way government produces inflation. The most common ways of monetary expansion are when the central banks purchase securities in the market with newly printed money or when they buy government bonds directly. According to economist F.A. Hayek[23], the first receivers of the new money are the ones that end up winning, as they can purchase goods at the previous prices, at the expense of the later receivers of the newly printed money. When the new money expands through society, it raises prices and distorts the productive structure, as not all prices rise equally and at the same time. One of the main functions of money, according to economist Ludwig von Mises, is that it allows for economic calculation, which is crucial for a society to invest resources efficiently. With the distorted price relations, economic calculation cannot be performed correctly, so many resources end up malinvested. Hayek states that the new productive structure will not represent the real needs of the consumers, and therefore it must be readjusted via a recession.

The economists of the modern monetary theory claim that inflation is not damaging to the economy if it does not constitute a rise in prices due to the increase in productivity. Even if the prices do not change nominally, inflation constitutes a transfer in purchasing power from the people to the government, as otherwise, people would have been able to buy more goods with the same amount of money.

The reason money retains its value in time is because people expect it to be able to purchase a similar quantity of goods in the future as it can in the present. When governments inflate their monetary supply very often, people begin anticipating a decrease in the purchasing power of money and act accordingly. Because people believe money will be worth less tomorrow than it is worth today, they increase their spending and diminish their savings. When this tendency continues for some time, people start spending the money they have as soon as they can and adjust their valuation of money taking into account the expected inflation, to the point that the prices of the goods in the present reflect the future lower expected value of money, and no one has enough bills to pay for them. This phenomenon is called hyperinflation and constitutes the destruction of the monetary system.

THE BOOM AND BUST CYCLE

In 1936, during the Great Depression, economist John Maynard Keynes published The General Theory of Employment, Interest and Money. This caused a major shift in economic thought and, even after 85 years, it has remained highly influential among economists and politicians. The main purpose of this book was to explain the business cycle and provide a solution to economic crises that is centered on macroeconomic aggregates. It also provided the theoretical support politicians needed to justify government spending, inflation, budgetary deficits, and economic manipulation.

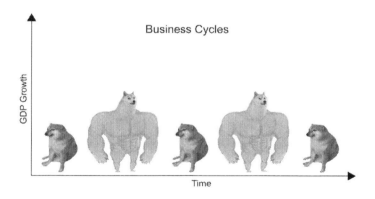

Figure 2. Business cycles

The business cycle can be briefly defined as the fluctuation between expansion and contraction of economic activity over a period of time. Keynes explains this phenomenon by the variations in the rate of investment, which fluctuates because of the marginal efficiency of capital, which can be defined as the expected profits of new investments[25]. In a market economy, entrepreneurs decide to invest or not based on the expected profitability of the ventures.

Keynes understood business cycles as fluctuations over time of employment, income, and output. According to him, income and output depend on the volume of employment. In Keynesian economics, employment is determined by the marginal efficiency of capital, the rate of interest, and the propensity to consume. As the latter two are stable in the short term, the marginal efficiency of capital is the main determinant of the volume of employment, and therefore, its variation is the cause of economic fluctuations[25].

According to Keynes, the expansion phase of the business cycle is the result of a high marginal efficiency of capital[25]. During this phase, businessmen have positive expectations and make many investments. Employment and income levels are high, and they keep rising with each additional investment made. The expansive phase eventually reaches a peak, in which the marginal efficiency of capital diminishes. This happens because the cost of production of capital assets increases due to the shortage of labor and materials, and also because the abundance of consumer goods produced lowers profits. The optimism businessmen had at the beginning of the economic expansion soon turns into pessimism, and the marginal efficiency of capital plummets, as their previously made investments now seem unprofitable. The cut in investments creates unemployment, which causes a cumulative decrement in income. Then, the economy enters a phase of depression that lasts until businessmen regain confidence, which happens when the marginal efficiency of capital increases. Keynes says this will happen when the excess stock of consumer goods gets exhausted and the durable capital wears out. This will generate a scarcity of consumer and capital goods, which will consequently raise their prices and increase the expectation of profits.

The solution Keynes proposed to economic depressions is based on the application of countercyclical measures by the government. In Keynes' view, during an expansion, the government must raise taxes and lower public spending as a way to cool down the growth, and during a contraction, the government must lower interest rates, increase public spending and print more money. In the event of a crisis, the lowering of the private demand for labor can be compensated by an increase in government spending, maintaining the employment levels stable. The expansive policies advocated by Keynes were implemented by Franklin D. Roosevelt with the New

Deal and have been the preferred option of many politicians ever since.

One of the main faults of Keynes' theory is that it doesn't explain the determinants of the marginal efficiency of capital. Keynes bases all his theory on the fluctuation of the marginal efficiency of capital but doesn't explain what causes it. He describes the phases of the business cycle and proposes solutions to economic crisis but is unable to get to its causes, even suggesting "animal spirits" as one of them[26]. Conventional wisdom states that you must treat the cause, not the symptoms, but this is the opposite of what Keynes does with his recipe of countercyclical measures, completely ignoring the causes of economic crises. According to Keynes, an irrational fall in aggregate demand is the cause of depressions and the government must correct it by more spending. His theory never considers the effects that monetary policy can have on the productive structure of capital.

Another great fault of the Keynesian theory is that it ignores the structure of production and the influence prices have on it[28]. As pointed out by economist Ludwig von Mises, prices are fundamental for economic calculation, as they enable society to decide in what to spend its limited resources. Keynes considered capital to be homogenous, which oversimplifies the nature of capital and ignores the information contained in the relation between prices[27]. An alteration in the relation of prices can distort the process of economic calculation and result in a misallocation of resources. Typically, the resources of a certain society are allocated in such a way that it procures the fulfillment of the wants and needs of that society. If, for example, a society has a high demand for winter clothes, then businesses should have to exist to provide that service. If the amount of businesses that sell winter clothes is insufficient, there would be scarcity, which would raise the prices of those products, increasing the profit margin and motivating more entrepreneurs to invest in selling winter clothes. If the supply exceeds the demand, prices would fall, reducing the profit margin and slowly driving capital away from those businesses. Over the long term, there exists a dynamic equilibrium that guarantees that society's desire for winter clothes will be fulfilled. Entrepreneurs can decide when to invest and in which businesses because of the information obtained from the profit margins. The problem with inflation is that it distorts these profit margins. Keynesian economists argue that inflation, an increase in the supply of money, helps promote economic growth, but they don't take into account its effect in the relation of prices. According to economist Jesus Huerta de Soto[28], monetary changes are never neutral. The new money always enters the economy in some very specific points and is spent on some determined goods and services, and it is only with time that it expands to the rest of the productive structure. A consequence of this is that some prices will be modified earlier than others, which consequently modifies the allocation of resources. Some businesses that would have been unprofitable in normal circumstances become profitable with the issuance of new money, and laborers that would otherwise be unemployed find jobs in artificially profitable sectors. Let's suppose, for example, that a certain monetary policy directs the newly printed money towards the construction sector, by lending it to real estate developers at very low interest rates. In the short term, the profit margin of the real estate projects would increase, not because of the desire for more buildings by the society, but because of the monetary policies. To the eyes of entrepreneurs, real estate would seem more profitable than other ventures, such as selling winter clothes, so they would allocate more resources to that sector and less to others. This is the consequence of a distortion of profit margins that does not permit an efficient allocation of resources. In the medium and long term, society would have an excess of construction projects and not enough winter clothes.

The effects of monetary policies on the business cycle can also be analyzed from the consumption-investment perspective. A society that values present consumption very highly will probably spend a considerable amount of its resources on consumption goods and save little money for investment. The interest rates in this society will be high and therefore the investment in capital goods, which will only be profitable after some years, will be low. A society with low time preference will save a considerable portion of its resources, so the interest rate will be low and many investments will be undertaken in capital goods industries. In each case, the productive structure adapts to best serve the needs of society, balancing the ratio between investments in capital goods and consumer goods. This ratio can artificially be modified by governments with their monetary policies. Jesus Huerta de Soto[28] points out that new money enters the economy because of inflation and an artificial lowering of interest rates. The low interest rates and increased volume of money result in an increase in investment spending in relation to consumption, and this distorts the indicators that guide businessmen when deciding on what to invest. With lower interest rates, some investments that previously were unprofitable now seem profitable. The result of this is an increase of spending on capital goods, or goods that are used in the production of other goods. This raises the prices of productive factors, which leads businessmen to look for production methods that require less labor. The demand for natural resources also rises as a consequence of more investments made in capital goods industries. Businesses that sell consumer goods see their costs rise without an increase in prices, which lowers their profits. This causes some of the resources invested in consumer goods industries to be moved to the more profitable capital goods industries, a process that continues for a long period of time.

According to Jesus Huerta de Soto[28], the increase in profits made by the capital goods industries generates a higher demand for consumer goods, which consequently increases their prices. The previous reallocation of resources from consumer goods to capital goods caused the consumer goods supply to decrease, a factor that also contributes to the rise in prices. This causes the consumer goods industries to start being more profitable in relation to the capital goods industries. Some of the resources previously invested in capital goods industries must be reallocated to the consumer goods industries. As prices rise, the real salaries become lower and the demand for labor of consumer goods becomes higher. The necessary reallocation of resources from capital goods industries to consumer goods industries generates great losses in the process as capital is not so easily adaptable[28]. Businesses in which too many resources were invested, such as construction, must be halted as they were only profitable because of the low interest rates. Many of the investments that were made in capital goods cannot be taken to completion, because they would require more resources than are available at the moment. As a result of an excess of production of capital goods and a lack of production of consumer goods, the economic depression starts.

With the start of a crisis, unemployment rises in industries related to capital goods, and because of the inflexibility of the labor market, it takes a significant amount of time for all the people who lose their jobs to be reabsorbed into other industries. Inflation could be used at the beginning of the expansive phase of the business cycle to artificially generate economic growth, but as people begin expecting it and start losing faith in the purchasing power of money, it loses its expansive capability. Governments can print their way into a crisis, but not out of it. If governments persist in using inflation just to delay the recession, hyperinflation will ensue, only worsening the situation.

At the end of the expansive phase of the business cycle, the productive structure of capital was not fit to satisfy the needs of society, because the artificially modified profit margins did not reflect the real desires of people, causing a misallocation of resources. A depression is a process of healthy reallocation of resources, which must be facilitated by governments by not interfering with damaging monetary policies[28]. Further inflation or fiscal stimulus would only make the recession longer and bigger, as it would create uncertainty and the malinvestment of more resources15. After a long phase of monetary expansion, inflation and malinvestment of resources, a correction in the form of a depression becomes not only necessary, but inevitable. When the depression has passed, the productive structure of capital should reflect the needs and desires of society and a phase of healthy and balanced economic growth should ensue.

THE FAILURE OF FIAT CURRENCIES

Fiat currencies are a form of money issued by governments that is not backed by any physical asset, such as gold or silver. In other words, they are money because governments say so. But even the coercive power of governments is not enough to give value to something worthless, so the value of fiat currencies isn't really determined by law, but by the trust people place in it. Money can be useful as a medium of exchange, a unit of account, and a store of value, and in ideal circumstances, the paper bills printed by governments should be able to serve these three functions well. In this way, governments become providers of a very important service that is essential for the functioning of the economy, the issuance of money.

Each government has a monopoly over the issuance of its own currency, and it is because of this monopolistic power that most problems arise. If all governments were responsible and respectful of individual liberties, they would limit their functions to issuing the currency and no more. They wouldn't print extra money, except to replace worn-out bills, and they wouldn't manipulate the economy with intrusive monetary policies; but, as there are few limits to what governments can do, this is rarely the case. The monopolistic power over money often gets abused to the advantage of politicians and the detriment of the people.

The purchasing power of money is derived from the relation of supply and demand for it. The quantity of money in an economy, then, is not very relevant, as prices will be set in relation to this amount, but a sudden change in it can cause great havoc. In a gold-backed currency, the amount of new gold that can be mined every year is small in comparison to the existing stock. Only in rare historical events, such as the discovery of America or the gold rush in California, inflation has been a problem with the gold standard, due to the increase in the supply of money. With fiat currencies the opposite is true. Increasing the supply of money is as easy as putting the printing machines to work. This leaves the people at a great disadvantage, as the only thing they can do is hope that the government doesn't decide to abuse this power. When new currency is printed, not only does the value of each unit of money decreases, but the purchasing power gets redistributed. A portion of the purchasing power that was previously held by the people gets transferred to the government, acting inflation as a passive way of taxation. This is why inflation is often preferred by politicians, as printing new money is easier than approving new taxes and has a lower political cost.

A moderate rate of inflation is somewhat

harmful to the economy but can be sustainable. The real problem arises when governments begin printing even more and more money so, as described in previous chapters, people's valuations adjust to the future expected value of money, producing hyperinflation. This makes the money essentially worthless and causes great economic destruction, as the official currency is no longer useful as neither a unit of account nor a store of value.

The monetary equivalent of printing new money when the currency was backed by a commodity is debasement. This usually happened when rulers combined gold and silver coins with a cheaper metal to increase the quantity of coins, decreasing their value. Debasement also happened with paper money when banks issued more deposit notes than the amount of gold they had stored, decreasing the value of the notes.

There are several historical examples that are useful to illustrate the consequences of printing a lot of money. After the end of the First World War, the newly created Weimar Republic was saddled with debt, due to all the money they had borrowed to pay for the war and the economic sanctions that were imposed on them in the Treaty of Versailles. As the German government was unable to raise all the money to pay debts via taxation, they had to devalue the currency. Because of the massive increase in money supply, the German Mark, which was no longer backed by gold, soon lost most of its value. A loaf of bread that could be bought for 163 marks in 1922 costed 200,000,000,000 marks in November 1923[29]. To stop the hyperinflation, the government had to issue a new gold-backed currency in 1923, called the Rentenmark.

A scenario similar to that of post-war Germany was seen in Zimbabwe more recently. In the 1980s, president Robert Mugabe instituted a land reform redistributing farming properties among many people that lacked the technical knowledge to grow crops. This resulted in a significant decline in production. In 1998, despite the economic crisis the country was in, Mugabe decided to send troops to fight in the Second Congo War[30]. These measures resulted in a significant reduction of the country's monetary reserves. In the early 2000s, Zimbabwe's government started having difficulties paying for public spending. Against the advice of economists, Mugabe instructed the Reserve Bank of Zimbabwe to print more money to pay for the expenses[30]. This decision had terrible consequences. The Zimbabwean inflation rate, which was 112% in 2001, rose to 1281% by 2006 and reached 79.600.000.000% in November 2008[31]. People had to begin using foreign currencies to protect themselves from hyperinflation, which eventually became the government's solution in 2009 when they stopped printing Zimbabwean dollars and urged people to use the currency of their choice. In 2019 the government reintroduced a national currency, but made the same mistakes as before. As a result of this, the annual inflation rate was higher than 700% in 2020[32].

Venezuelan president Nicolas Maduro made the same mistakes as Robert Mugabe. For the last decades, the socialist policies of Venezuela's government have crippled the economy and increased government spending. The government's income depended heavily on oil exports, but when oil prices dropped, the government had to print more money to make up for the losses. The increase in the supply of bolivars caused its purchasing power to plummet. The Venezuelan Central Bank registered inflation rates of 274% in 2016, 863% in 2017, and 130.060% in 2018[33]. In 2019 the IMF estimated Venezuelan inflation at 10 million percent[34].

Figure 3. Inflation doge

As discussed in previous chapters, hyperinflation has been a common phenomenon throughout history. The massive increase in the supply of devalued silver denarii was one of the causes of the deep economic crisis which eventually led the Roman Empire to its collapse. A similar situation happened in China during the Yuan dynasty when they began printing large quantities of unbacked paper money. Hyperinflation, more than a problem of fiat currencies, is a problem of government. As history has proven, when governments are given the chance, they tend to abuse the power they have over the monopoly of money. The problem with fiat currencies is that they require the population to place a disproportionate amount of trust in governments. Governments that minted metallic currencies also had this problem, as they could debase the coins causing inflation. Even if most governments were rightful and trustworthy, over a long period of time there will likely be one bad government that will abuse its power over money, causing high levels of inflation and an economic crisis. A better currency, therefore, would be one that does not require people to blindly trust the government with the monopoly over money, because this trust has often been violated.

Another great danger of fiat currencies is the control they give governments over the economy. A country with a monopoly over its currency can decide when and how much money to print, which can be very dangerous. Whenever the economy is not growing as fast as politicians think it should they decide to print more money and lower the interest rates so that employment levels rise and the economy grows more rapidly. This leads to overinvestment in unprofitable businesses and a misallocation of capital, which results in a distortion of the productive structure of capital. The economic expansion which was started with cheap money policies by the government eventually ends in a depression. Governments are only able to do this because of the control they have over money. If the government wasn't able to print more money at will or lower interest rates to promote spending, artificial booms would not happen, and neither the subsequent busts. Whenever there is a minor decline in GDP growth the government's response is to lower interest rates and print more money. What this does is prevent necessary market corrections, without which the misallocation of capital continues. This eventually leads to a massive market correction in the form of a big economic crisis, that could have been avoided if the small corrections were made in time.

A natural consequence of fiat currencies is the existence of institutions that have control over them, or in other words, central banks. One of the main functions of central banks all over the world, apart from printing money, is acting as lenders of last resort. Whenever a bank has liquidity problems the central bank gives it money so that it won't go bankrupt. This is deeply damaging for the financial system as it creates a moral hazard, encouraging banks to take more risks than what is prudent[35]. The present situation can be compared to a gambler that receives all the benefits from the bets he wins but gets reimbursed every time he has losses. As banks are insured by the government, they gamble with the money of the people, and when they lose, the government bails them out because they are "too big to fail"[35].

The artificial manipulation of interest rates and government insurance of banks were two of the main causes of the 2008 financial crisis. In the years previous to the crisis, the government lowered interest rates to promote economic growth[36]. This made investments in real estate seem more profitable. Banks saw an opportunity to make large profits in the housing bubble, so they kept pumping money into that sector despite the significant risk. When the bubble burst the banks faced significant trouble, but most of them were bailed out by the government using taxpayers' money.

The only logical conclusion of this nefarious monetary system is economic collapse. Whenever politicians are coming short of money to fund their populist proposals, they can just print more money, robbing the people of a portion of their purchasing power. Whenever a president wants to increase his approval ratings, he just orders the central bank to start pumping money into the economy, which in the short and medium term will generate economic acceleration helping his purpose, but in the long term will create a depression, hopefully when he isn't in office anymore.

The current monetary system is not set to help

the people, ease transactions, increase efficiency and generate long-term economic growth, but to help politicians further their causes and help their campaign donors. There is no guarantee that the government will not abuse its power and take advantage of the situation. Some politicians even argue that the cheap money policies they implement are really in the best interest of the people, using the theories of Keynesians and modern monetary theorists as justification.

There is a popular saying that says: "Man is the only animal that trips twice over the same stone", and it seems to reflect perfectly the present monetary situation. Governments, with their control over currencies, have created several economic depressions bringing great misfortune to the people. The solution to this crisis has almost always been the same: abandoning bad investments, decreasing waste, reallocating capital, and when everything gets better, trusting in governments again just to perpetuate the cycle. This situation cannot be solved by electing trustworthy leaders and central bankers, as even the best of men can be corrupted, or electing only the smartest people to office, as even they can be fooled by fancy economic theories (MMT). The only viable solution to avoid the next big financial crisis is to stop trusting the government with the monopoly over money. Governments might be beneficial to other causes, but history has proven that controlling money, inflation, and interest rates are not one of them. A new monetary system must emerge to replace the fiat standard, one that is free from government intervention, decentralized, and trustless.

Cryptocurrencies

In 2008, during the midst of the financial crisis, subscribers to the gmane.comp.encryption.general mailing list received an email from an unknown person under the pseudonym of Satoshi Nakamoto[37]. In the letter, Satoshi described a new monetary system named Bitcoin, based on cryptography, that had anonymity and decentralization as its main attributes. In its whitepaper38 Bitcoin is described as a "purely peer-to-peer version of electronic cash that would allow online payments to be sent directly from one party to another without going through a financial institution". This new form of money was launched in 2009, becoming, the first decentralized cryptocurrency. In its first years, Bitcoin was only mined by a small group of enthusiasts, and it was only used for a transaction until 2010, obtaining economic value. Two years after the birth of Bitcoin, other cryptocurrencies were created, such as Litecoin, which is a fork of Bitcoin. The next year Dogecoin was launched, which is a fork of Litecoin. In 2014 Ethereum was created, which incorporated smart contracts into the blockchain, and many more cryptocurrencies have been created ever since.

Cryptocurrencies are digital assets designed to fulfill the functions of money. These currencies use cryptographic protocols to encrypt transaction records, control the creation of new coins and verify the ownership and transfer of money[39]. This information is stored in the ledger. Contrary to fiat currencies, cryptocurrencies are not created by governments or central banks, but by private entities. Similar to fiat currencies, these digital tokens are not backed by any commodity. They are valuable because of the subjective valuation of the people, and the trust they have in them. Another crucial characteristic of most cryptocurrencies is decentralization, meaning no single entity has control over the ledger, as it is distributed.

According to the computer scientist Jan Lansky[40], the following six characteristics are necessary for a system to be considered a cryptocurrency:

1. The system is decentralized, meaning it does not have a central authority.

2. The system keeps a register of the token units and their owner.

3. The system defines the protocol for the creation of new units and their ownership.

4. Ownership of the units can only be proven cryptographically.

5. The system allows for transactions in which the ownership of a cryptographic unit is changed, and requires its current owner to prove its ownership.

6. The cryptographic units cannot be double spent, meaning an individual cannot transfer units that he has already transferred away.

The three main characteristics that separate cryptocurrencies from fiat currencies are: independence from central authority, pseudo-anonymity, and double-spending attack protection[40]. Cryptocurrencies are pseudo-anonymous because the real name of the owner of each wallet cannot be easily known, but negligence from the user or the use of additional data (KYC policies) can lead to identifying users. The registry of all transaction data is stored in the blockchain, so criminal investigation agencies can use specialized software to track the movement of coins to certain addresses suspect of illegal activities. The only way to change the consensus rules of a cryptocurrency system is by the consensus of the majority of the crypto operators. No central authority, such as a central bank, can change the rules by which a cryptocurrency is governed. Because of the lack of a central authority, cryptocurrencies cannot be regulated with coercion. Only the users of the system can voluntarily modify the rules by which the system is governed by achieving consensus.

A key concept for understanding cryptocurrencies is the blockchain, the database in which the ownership of each cryptographic unit is stored. The blockchain is a shared database in which the registry of transactions and the ownership of assets of a system are kept[41]. Once the data is stored, it is unmodifiable and can only be accessed by the users of the network. The blockchain, as its name implies, is a chain-like database in which blocks of information are linked together. This system makes the information stored unmodifiable. When a block is filled and added to the blockchain, it is marked with a timestamp and is as if it were written in stone[41]. All users of the system can access the blockchain simultaneously to check the ownership of assets. Most cryptocurrencies use a blockchain to manage the ownership of the coins. Whenever a new transaction is made, it is validated by a network of peer-to-peer computers. When transactions are confirmed to be legitimate, they are grouped into a block, and when the block is full, it gets chained into the blockchain, where all the history of transactions is permanently stored.

A common characteristic of most blockchains is decentralization. Typically, business databases are controlled by one entity and are stored in a certain building. With decentralization, the blockchain is stored in thousands of computers all over the world. These computers, controlled by separate individuals, are called nodes, and every time a new block is added to the chain it gets stored in every node[41]. Every individual with a node can access the registry of all transactions of a cryptocurrency. This means that anyone can view all the coins being transferred and the addresses involved in the transaction. If a node has an error or stops working, the blockchain remains intact as all the other nodes are still running. If a user tries to maliciously modify the registry of transactions in a node, all the information gets cross-referenced from the other nodes in the network so the tampered node can easily be spotted.

For a change to be implemented in the protocol that governs the blockchain, the majority of the computing power of the network would have to accept the changes. This is one of the factors that contribute to the security of cryptocurrencies. All blocks are added chronologically to the blockchain. Each block contains its own hash, the hash of the previous block in the chain, and a timestamp. A hash code is a computational function that turns data into a string of letters and numbers[39]. The same set of data always generates the same hash code, and once the hash is generated, it cannot be reversed to access the data that generated it. If even a minuscule part of the data is altered, the hash changes completely. If a user tries to modify his copy of the blockchain to alter the registry of transactions, it would differ from all the other copies. When the blockchain gets cross-referenced from the other nodes in the network, the tampered node can easily be spotted and the changes are rejected. The only way to modify the blockchain is if the meddled node were to become the majority node. For this to happen, the hacker would need to have control of at least 51% of the computing power of the network. With any big network, this labor would be extremely expensive, and even if the hacker could successfully modify the registry of transactions, the users of the network would notice. They would then do a fork to a new version of the network with the original blockchain. The original network would lose most of its value as people wouldn't trust it anymore, so the hacker would have control over worthless assets, disincentivizing, even more, any attempt to hack the network. The previous situation can be exemplified by the 2016 hack of Ethereum Classic, which ended with a fork into the current Ethereum network.

The process by which transactions of a cryptocurrency are verified is called mining. Miners work as the auditors of every transaction[39]. This helps prevents the double-spending problem. When a person wants to make a transaction to another person, he signs a digital message authorizing the coins to be sent. The receiver has no way of knowing if the coins have already been transferred to another person. Cryptocurrencies solve this problem by conducting all transfers in a common place, the blockchain. If a transaction has already been made with some coins, it can be checked in the blockchain and any attempt to double spend those coins would be invalid. A consensus order is followed verifying transactions[39]. Once an order has been established, any subsequent order trying to double-spend the same coins would be rejected. What miners do is to verify that all transaction orders are legitimate and then add them to the blockchain. In most cryptocurrencies, mining is also the only way new coins are created. For every transaction made a small fee is charged to reward the miners. Miners are also rewarded by the release of new coins. Each cryptocurrency establishes in its protocols how many new coins are created per block. For example, one Bitcoin block is added to the blockchain every 10 minutes, and the miner gets rewarded with 6.25 Bitcoins plus the transaction fees. In its protocols, it is established that Bitcoin rewards will be halved every 4 years. With Dogecoin, the block interval is of 1 minute and the miners are rewarded with 10.000 coins. The rewards that are paid are what incentivizes miners to verify transactions and keep the network secure.

Verifying the transactions is not enough for a miner to get rewarded. To deter malicious use of computing power, validating systems are used to make mining more costly. The most used ones are proof of work and proof of stake. Proof of work (PoW), which is used by Dogecoin and Bitcoin, requires the miners to use computing power to solve complex mathematical problems. For each block, a target hash is set and the first miner that generates a hash equal or lower to the target earns the rewards[42]. Since being the first miner to guess the correct hash is highly improbable, miners usually gather in mining pools that join computing power to increase their chances of success and distribute the rewards. Any attempt to validate fraudulent transactions would generate economic losses to the attacker as the block would not be accepted by other miners. The main criticism towards proof of work mining is that the process is very energy-intensive. The second most common validating protocol is proof of stake (PoS) and is used by other cryptocurrencies such as Cardano. In this system, validators can verify transactions based on the number of coins they own. Each node has to deposit a certain amount of the network's tokens into a network at stake, which is something similar to a security deposit[43]. For each new block, a node is randomly chosen to validate all the transactions in a block. The chance of each node being selected depends on the size of the staking, which is why small owners usually join staking pools. The proponents of a proof of stake system argue that it is more secure than the proof of work system. To make a 51% attack in a PoW validated cryptocurrency the attacker has to control 51% of all the computing power in the network, which would be very costly, but in the PoS system, the attacker has to own at least 51% of the staked coins, which would cost even more. This would require massive investments by any attacker, and even if the attack would go through, the value of the hacked cryptocurrency would plummet, generating the attacker heavy economic losses. The PoS system not only makes a 51% attack very costly but also very unappealing.

One of the biggest advantages of blockchain is that it removes third-parties from the equation. Transfers of money are made directly over the blockchain, without the need of a bank or other financial institutions. This makes transactions way cheaper than traditional methods. A Dogecoin transaction, for example, can be made for less than 20 cents of a dollar in fees and takes only a couple of minutes. A bank transfer can cost several dollars when done to an external account and take up to several hours to process. An international wire transfer can cost as much as 45 USD and take more than a day to be processed, but with blockchain, it can be done as easily, as fast, and as cheap as any other transfer.

In an age of increasing government surveillance, the blockchain also offers its users more privacy and security than traditional banks. All transfers made over a public blockchain can be traceable, but it can be very hard to establish the ownership of the coins if they were purchased anonymously. Some cryptocurrencies as Monero even offer complete privacy, making transactions untraceable. The fact that cryptocurrencies are decentralized and anonymous makes it almost impossible for authoritarian governments to freeze the savings of political dissidents. This, in addition, increases freedom of speech, as those who decide to speak against a certain government don't have to fear financial persecution and the confiscation of their assets.

Cryptocurrencies are also way more accessible than traditional bank accounts. Opening a bank account can take several weeks, requires an identification and to fill various forms. Opening a crypto wallet is as easy as downloading a computer or mobile app. This has led to the adoption of cryptocurrencies as a medium of exchange by the population of some third-world countries where access to financial institutions is thorny. Over the past years, crypto has surged in the African continent[44], especially in countries like Ghana, Kenya, Nigeria, South Africa, and Zimbabwe, having the last one a long history of monetary instability. Many businesses in these places have already started accepting cryptocurrencies as a form of payment, and this trend is only expected to grow in the following years.

The biggest advantage of cryptocurrencies is that they can break the monopoly government has over money. As mentioned in previous chapters, this monopoly was established because of the advantages of having a common medium of exchange that everyone could trust and accept, but governments soon began abusing their power. The debasement of currency was a common practice of governments in antiquity, and with the creation of paper money, inflation has been even more common. Having the monopoly over money has allowed governments to steal purchasing power from the people through inflation without the need to charge more taxes. In some of the worst cases, this has even led to hyperinflation, such as the one in Germany in 1923, which created the economic conditions which led to the rise of Nazism, or the one in Venezuela in recent history that has provoked a massive exodus of people from that country. Even when governments have been able to avoid hyperinflation, the monopoly they possess over money has been one of the main causes of economic crashes. Whenever politicians think the economy isn't growing as fast as it should, they order central banks to begin expansive monetary policies. The most common of these policies are lowering the discount rate, lowering the monetary reserves, and quantitative easing, which is a massive purchase of government bonds and other financial assets by central banks with newly printed money. In the long term, this will lower interest rates and benefit the recipients of the new money, as they can purchase goods for their pre-inflation price. The lowering of interest rates, without an increase in the savings of society, leads to an increase in investments in some industries that only seem profitable because of the artificially low interest rates. Expansive monetary policies can't go on forever, and when people realize that resources have been dangerously misallocated, the bubble bursts, and an economic crisis ensues. This happened with the 2008 financial crisis, after years of the Clinton and Bush administration pumping money into the economy and maintaining artificially low interest rates. This led to a massive misallocation of resources into the housing market, which ultimately collapsed causing the crisis. The 2008 crisis could have been avoided if the government didn't conduct such reckless expansive monetary policies, or, even better, if it didn't have the option to conduct such reckless policies. The United States government has not learned the lesson, approving multitrillion-dollar stimulus packages in 2020 and 2021. For future crises to be avoided there seems to be only one solution. If history has proven anything it is that governments cannot be trusted with the monopoly over money. For safe and stable economic growth to be attained, without booms and busts, money must be democratized, and currently, the best way to achieve this is through cryptocurrencies. In the blockchain, the community has control over the policies they decide to enact, and they can only be implemented by consensus. Cryptocurrencies transfer power away from governments to the people. Since cryptocurrencies remove the government monopoly of money, prevent business cycles, give more control and freedom to the people, and provide cheaper, safer, and more private transactions than fiat currencies, a future where cryptocurrencies take over the world financial system is inexorable. The main obstacles to this end are governments because they are the ones that would lose the most, and they may try to delay the adoption of crypto with increasing taxes and regulations, but this ongoing monetary revolution is not set to happen because of governments, but despite them.

THE CASE FOR DOGECOIN

Dogecoin is an open-source peer-to-peer digital currency, favored by Shiba Inus worldwide[45]. It was created by software engineers Jackson Palmer and Billy Markus (aka Shibetoshi Nakamoto). Before the creation of Dogecoin, Jackson Palmer was an Adobe Systems product manager in Sydney Australia. After seeing all the buzz around Bitcoin and the emerging cryptocurrency technology, he purchased the domain name dogecoin.com, in which he set a splash screen with the logo of the coin to satirize the situation. Billy Markus, a software engineer at IBM who wanted to create a cryptocurrency, contacted Palmer after discovering the Dogecoin webpage, asking permission to build the software behind the real coin. Dogecoin was officially released on December 6, 2013. It takes its name and logo from its mascot, the doge, which became popular because of the online meme featuring a Shiba Inu, a Japanese breed of dog, captioned with interior monologues in Comic Sans font. Dogecoin is meant to be a fun and friendly cryptocurrency, that provides instant money transfers and is free from traditional banking institutions.

Figure 4. Dogecoin

Dogecoin is based on the source-code of Luckycoin and Litecoin, which are both based on Bitcoin. It is a proof of work cryptocurrency, meaning transactions are validated by miners that use computing power to verify transactions and solve complex mathematical operations to get the rewards. Unlike Bitcoin, Dogecoin uses the scrypt technology in its proof of work algorithm and not SHA-256. Some Bitcoin miners use Application-Specific Integrated Circuits (ASICs), a specialized form of hardware that makes mining more efficient. The consequence of this is that mining has become less rewarding for common individuals that use GPU mining, which is way more accessible. Scrypt was designed so that it makes more difficult the use of ASICs, leveling the technological field and encouraging more users to participate in the mining process.

Dogecoin has a target time of one minute per block, shorter than Litecoin's 2,5 minutes and Bitcoin's 10 minutes. The difficulty readjustment is done after every block. This is done to keep the mining rate constant over the short-term variations in networking hashing rate and the long-term increase in computing power. A reward of 10.000 Dogecoin is paid to the miners for every block that is added to the blockchain. Unlike Bitcoin's and Litecoin's rewards, which halve every four years, Dogecoin's rewards have been permanently fixed at ten thousand coins per block since the 600.000[th] block. This is done to encourage miners to verify transactions and to secure the network.

One of the main characteristics of any usable currency is that it can easily be transferred from one person to another. Fiat currencies have achieved a high level of transactability with all the debit and credit card systems and online payment methods like PayPal. The main issue with fiat transfers is their high cost, as banks usually charge a large commission for processing payments. Most of these transfers can take several hours to process or even several days if the transfer is international. The benefits of these fiat money transfer systems are mostly perceived in developed countries.

Bitcoin represents an advancement over antiquated wire transfers, but as a solution for an easily transactable currency, it is far from ideal. The average fee paid for a Bitcoin transaction[46] in the first quarter of 2021 was more than $10. Due to the time interval set for Bitcoin's block time transactions can only be verified every 10 minutes, and they may take even more depending on the congestion of the network and the fees paid. If Bitcoin were to be adopted by society as a currency, its use would be very inconvenient, especially for small transactions and day-to-day use. This has led many of its supporters to stop advocating for it as a medium of exchange and instead promote it as a store of value. The people that previously said that Bitcoin is the new dollar now say it is the new gold. Dogecoin, which was originally created as a parody of Bitcoin, is a far better solution for the money transfer problem. Dogecoin's block time is of just one minute. This means that transactions can be verified in as few as sixty seconds. Even if the network is congested and transfers take up to several minutes, this is still way faster than Bitcoin and orders of magnitude faster than conventional wire transfers which can take more than a day. The transfer costs of Dogecoin were on average less than $0.15 during the first quarter of 2021[47], way lower than those of other cryptocurrencies such as Bitcoin or Ethereum.

Dogecoin, like most other cryptocurrencies, is available to every person in the world that has access to the internet. This is a major advantage over traditional financial services that depend on fiat currencies. Opening a bank account can be difficult in many underdeveloped countries, especially for people that live in rural areas or lack identifications. By 2017, a total of 1.7 billion adults didn't have access to a bank account[48]. The majority of these people live in underdeveloped countries like South Sudan, Central African Republic, Afghanistan, Niger, and Madagascar, where more than 80% of all adults remain unbanked. Dogecoin is a great opportunity for financial inclusion in underdeveloped countries. Opening a crypto wallet is as easy as downloading an app. People that previously didn't have access to financial services or loans could be able to receive cryptographic loans from people all over the world at very low fees. Micro-loan services, such as those provided by the Grameen bank, could be greatly expanded with Dogecoin, improving financial inclusion and increasing economic development, especially in third-world countries.

Many people in underdeveloped countries depend on money sent to them by family members that have emigrated to other countries looking for better-paying jobs. The remittances sent with services such as Western Union and Money Gram are usually subject to very high fees, but with Dogecoin these fees would be essentially zero. This can considerably increase the income of people in third-world countries by saving them a lot of money they previously spent on intermediaries. The use of Dogecoin for money transfers is not only cheaper and faster but is also more secure and reliable. Its implementation would benefit considerably the well-being of millions of people in third-world countries.

A criticism made to Dogecoin by many crypto investors is that its total supply does not have a hard cap, like Bitcoin that is limited to a total of 21 million coins. In early 2015 there were 100 billion Dogecoins in existence, and since then 5 billion coins have been added to the supply every year. These new coins minted are paid as a reward to miners at a rate of 10.000 coins per block mined, which happens every minute. Some people even argue that because Dogecoin's supply is not limited it will tend to infinity and it will be worthless, but this argument could not be more wrong. Only 5 billion coins can be minted annually, which means that as the supply grows every year, inflation will decrease. In the year 2021 Dogecoin's inflation rate was 4%, by 2030 it will be less than 3%, and by 2046 it will be 2%. In the year 2096 its annual inflation rate will be just 1%, and by 2140, the year the last Bitcoin will be mined, Dogecoin's inflation rate will be 0.69%. The 10.000 new coins minted every minute serve as a subsidy to miners to keep the network secure and the transaction fees low. Without it, one of two things could happen: either fees would skyrocket to pay the miners, or people would stop viewing mining as a profitable activity, making the network insecure. Because Bitcoin's supply is limited to a definite number of coins, investors view it as a scarce asset and invest in it expecting its value to rise as the supply becomes more limited. This has led to hoarding and price speculation, as people only buy it because they think its value will appreciate in the future, not because they intend to spend it. No one buys dollars as an investment, but rather they use them to buy stuff and invest in other assets. The opposite happens with Bitcoin, which is more of an investment than it is a currency. Although Dogecoin's inflation is very low the fact that its supply is not limited has kept speculative investors away from it, which may seem like something bad, but considering Dogecoin is a currency and not a speculative investment asset, it is something very good. The purpose of a currency is to facilitate transactions between people, not to be hoarded in a digital wallet expecting its value to double.

The main problems associated with fiat currencies inflation would be eliminated if the Dogecoin Standard were to be adopted. Governments can print more money because they have control over the central banks. When governments consistently print too much money, people begin adjusting to this phenomenon and they start accepting money for what its future purchasing power will be. The result of this is hyperinflation. Dogecoin completely nullifies the risk of hyperinflation, as its inflation rate is very low, fixed, and predictable. Not only this, but like most other cryptocurrencies, Dogecoin is also decentralized, which means that governments have no control over the amount of Dogecoins that are created every year and politicians can't print more money to pay for any new ludicrous government program they want to implement. Another problem associated with fiat currency inflation is that governments usually use it to artificially stimulate economic growth. In the short term, this generates a boom in the economy, but as explained in previous chapters, the result of government stimulus is the malinvestment of resources which eventually leads to a corrective phase, a recession. Substituting fiat currencies with Dogecoin virtually eliminates the business cycle, as most of the instruments governments use to manipulate the economy are tied to their control over currencies, and since Dogecoin is decentralized, they can't control it. Trusting politicians with the monopoly of any currency is very naive. Even if some are good and responsible, over the long term, politicians will be politicians. Eventually, they will abuse their power, print money, and lower interest rates to stimulate the economy, creating an economic crisis. With the adoption of the Dogecoin Standard, there is no need to trust politicians. Money will be used for the purposes it is meant for, as a medium of exchange, a store of value, and a unit of account, and not as a nefarious tool at the service of politicians to fulfill political agendas. The Dogecoin Standard might be the best chance society has to democratize money and to achieve stable and healthy economic growth.

Besides being a fast, secure, and decentralized cryptocurrency, Dogecoin can also be a force for good, as it has been many times in the past. The word DOGE has been used as an acronym by Dogecoin's creator Billy Markus for the motto "Do Only Good Everyday". This maxim truly reflects what Dogecoin is all about. Back in 2013, when Dogecoin was created, Bitcoin was involved in several controversies regarding its use for transactions associated with illegal activities. Dogecoins creators didn't want their cryptocurrency to be associated with criminal activities, so Dogecoin was promoted amongst its community as a coin for online tipping and charity. In 2014 the Jamaican Bobsled Team had qualified for the Winter Olympics in Sochi, but they didn't have the funds to attend the event. This came to the attention of the Dogecoin community, which started a fundraiser to support the team. In total, more than $36.000 were donated which helped secure the Jamaican's team participation in the event[49]. That same year, a campaign named Doge4Water was started by the Dogecoin community in collaboration with the non-profit organization Charity: Water. The campaign succeeded in fundraising more than $30.000 to buy two drilling wells in a remote region of Kenya to provide water access to locals. Since then, many more Dogecoins have been donated to charitable causes such as The Ocean Cleanup, which helps rid the ocean of plastic or Give Directly that supports people living in poverty. Charity is not an addendum to Dogecoin, but one of its main components. True to the spirit of Dogecoin, its community has proven time and time again their generosity. The worldwide adoption of the Dogecoin standard would only increase charitable donations all over the world as this coin is built around the concept of being generous and helping others out.

Figure 5. Dogesleigh

Photograph: secretlondon123 on flickr (CC-BY-SA)

Much has been said of the benefits that the adoption of the Dogecoin Standard would have towards a healthy economy and charitable causes, but it does not stop there. Replacing fiat currencies with Dogecoin could have a noticeable effect on the emotional wellbeing of the people. In his famous book Influence: The Psychology of Persuasion psychologist Robert Cialdini[50] talks about the principle of consistency. He states that people are motivated towards cognitive consistency and will change their attitudes, beliefs, and actions to achieve it. For example, if someone self-perceives as a healthy person it is more likely that he will behave in a healthy manner just to be consistent with his self-image. In 2019, psychologists Nicholas Coles, Jeff Larsen, and Heather Lench[51] analyzed data from 138 studies regarding the effects of facial feedback, or how emotions are influenced by facial expressions. The researchers concluded that facial expressions do have a small effect on feelings. Smiling can make you feel happier, scowling can make you feel angrier and frowning can make you sadder[51]. These results coincide with Cialdini's principle. The human brain relates a certain facial expression with its corresponding feelings and tries to act accordingly, achieving consistency. Dogecoin is a fun, friendly, and happy cryptocurrency. Because of the consistency principle, when people use Dogecoin they will tend to be more fun, happy, and friendly. Being angry and unfriendly is not part of the nature of Dogecoin, and therefore there would be a cognitive inconsistency in the brain of the users if they hold these feelings while using Dogecoin. Fiat currencies are often associated with greed and envy. Adopting the Dogecoin Standard would put an end to the negative connotations of money and replace them with positive things. Dogecoin could play a vital role in creating a more happy, fun, and friendly world.

Over the past decade cryptocurrencies have been taking over the world, but none of them yet has the strength to replace fiat currencies. Among cryptocurrencies, Dogecoin is the best suited to be used as a day-to-day currency. Bitcoin is expensive and slow to transfer; Litecoin is slower to transfer than Dogecoin and it has a limited supply, which favors hoarding, XRP is centralized and other cryptocurrencies like Ethereum, Cardano and Polkadot are not transactional currencies but platform currencies.

Replacing the fiat standard with the Dogecoin standard would be a great step towards the future of civilization. Fiat currencies are antiquated, they are slow and expensive to transfer, they give too much power to governments, allow high inflation, and favor the exclusion of a significant portion of humanity from access to financial services. Dogecoin is completely the opposite; it is fast and cheap to transfer, decentralized and trustless, has a fixed and decreasing inflation rate, supports the financial inclusion of excluded people, and nudges people towards a happier and friendlier behavior. The advantages Dogecoin has over any fiat currency are overwhelming. In the future years, Dogecoin will be used more and more, not as a speculative asset but as a medium of exchange. This process will not happen spontaneously. It requires the hard work and determination of all Dogecoin users. They have to relentlessly ask businesses to start accepting Dogecoin, pay in Dogecoin whenever it is possible, and convince family, friends, and neighbors of the advantages of using Dogecoin. With time more people will use Dogecoin as a medium of exchange, and more businesses will accept it for their products. This process implies the loss of power by central banks, as they will not be able to manipulate the monetary supply at will, so many governments might oppose the progressive adoption of Dogecoin, but as Victor Hugo said: "Nothing is more powerful than an idea whose time has come". Politicians are more reckless every day, and the solution to every new crisis seems to be to pump more money into the economy. This will inevitably lead fiat currencies to their collapse. With the fiat standard the people were hostage to the governments' monetary policies, but with the Dogecoin Standard people will regain their independence.

Imagine a world where money is democratized and not controlled by governments; a world in which there is no central bank-induced economic crisis; where transferring money is cheap and fast, regardless of the amount transferred or the location of the sender; a world in which everyone has access to financial services, even in the most underdeveloped countries; and in which the thought of money does not incite greed or envy, but generosity, friendliness, and happiness. This world is not as utopic as it seems, and replacing fiat currencies with Dogecoin might finally make it a reality. This world might seem distant, but Elon Musk, the technoking of Tesla, has already vaticinated it. The Dogecoin Standard taking over the global financial system is inevitable.

Figure 6. Dogecoin Standard

REFERENCES

1. J. Hur. The History of Money. BeBusinessed, [no date]. [Online] Available from: https://bebusinessed.com/history/the-history-of-money/ [Accessed 20 Feb 2021]

2. Provident Metals. The History of Money – A Walk through Time, [no date]. [Online] Available from: https://www.providentmetals.com/knowledge-center/precious-metals-resources/history-of-money.html [Accessed 20 Feb 2021]

3. A. Beattie. The History of Money. Investopedia, 2020. [Online] Available from: https://www.investopedia.com/articles/07/roots_of_money.asp [Accessed 21 Feb 2021]

4. M. Cartwright. Roman Coinage. World History Encyclopedia, 2018 [Online] Available from: https://www.ancient.eu/Roman_Coinage/ [Accessed 22 Feb 2021].

5. Intertrader. Did inflation collapse the Roman Empire? 2019 [Online] Available from: https://www.intertrader.com/en/blog/did-inflation-collapse-the-roman-empire/ [Accessed 23 Feb 2021]

6. K. Szczepasnki. The Invention of Paper Money. ThoughtCo, 2019. [Online] Available from: https://www.thoughtco.com/the-invention-of-paper-money-195167 [Accessed 23 Feb 2021]

7. J. H. Munro. Gold, Guilds and Governments. University of Toronto, 2002, p. 155. [Online] Available from: https://www.economics.utoronto.ca/munro5/JaarboekGuildsGovt.pdf [Accessed 24 Feb 2021]

8. J. H. Munro. Money, Prices, Wages, and 'Profit Inflation' in Spain, the Southern Netherlands, and England during the Price Revolution era. Revista Interdisciplinar, 2008, p. 15. [Online] Available from: https://www.economics.utoronto.ca/munro5/HistoriaEconomiaProfitInflation.pdf   [Accessed 25 Feb 2021]

9. International Bank Note Society. A History of Printed Money. [no date] [Online] Available from: https://www.theibns.org/ [Accessed 25 Feb 2021].

10. J. Huerta. Economic Recessions, Banking Reform, and the Future of Capitalism. 2010. [Online] Available from: https://mises.org/library/economic-recessions-banking-reform-and-future-capitalism [Accessed 27 Feb 2021]

11. E. Blessing. The Coinage Act of 1792. Investopedia, 2020 [Online] Available from: https://www.investopedia.com/terms/c/the-coinage-act-of-1972.asp [Accessed 27 Feb 2021]

12. T. McMahon. Confederate Inflation Rates. Inflation Data. [no date] [Online] Available from: https://inflationdata.com/articles/confederate-inflation/ [Accessed 28 Feb 2021]

13. R. Longley. The US Federal Reserve System. ThoughtCo, 2020. [Online] Available from: https://www.thoughtco.com/us-federal-reserve-system-3321733 [Accessed 1 Mar 2021]

14. R. L. Hetzel. The Evolution of U.S. Monetary Policy. Federal Reserve Bank of Richmond, 2017. [Online] Available from: https://www.richmondfed.org/publications/ [Accessed 1 Mar 2021]

15. I. M. Morehouse. Murray Rothbard's America's Great Depression. 2009 [Online] Available from: http://isaacmorehouse.com/ [Accessed 2 Mar 2021]

16. G. Smiley. The U.S. Economy in the 1920s. Marquette University, 2004. [Online] Available from: https://eh.net/encyclopedia/the-u-s-economy-in-the-1920s/ [Accessed 2 Mar 2021]

17. A. Hayes. Gold Reserve Act of 1934. Investopedia, 2021 [Online] Available from: https://www.investopedia.com/terms/g/gold-reserve-act-1934.asp [Accessed 2 Mar 2021].

18. J. Chen. Bretton Woods Agreement and System. Investopedia, 2010 [Online] Available from: https://www.investopedia.com/terms/b/brettonwoodsagreement.asp [Accessed 4 Mar 2021].

19. F. Holmes. The Gold Standard Ended 50 Years Ago. Federal Debt Has Only Exploded Since. Forbes, 2021 [Online] Available from: https://www.forbes.com/sites/greatspeculations/2021/01/25/the-gold-standard-ended-50-years-ago-federal-debt-has-only-exploded-since/ [Accessed 4 Mar 2021].

20. R. P. Murphy. Problems with the Cost Theory of Value. Mises Institute, 2011 [Online] Available from: https://mises.org/library/problems-cost-theory-value [Accessed 6 Mar 2021].

21. R. P. Murphy. Subjective-Value Theory. Mises Institute, 2011 [Online] Available from: https://mises.org/library/subjective-value-theory [Accessed 6 Mar 2021].

22. A. Hayes. Time-Preference Theory of Interest. Investopedia, 2021 [Online] Available from: https://www.investopedia.com/terms/t/time-preference-theory-of-interest.asp [Accessed 7 Mar 2021].

23. J. Huerta. Lecciones de economía lección 28 [no date] [Online] Available from: http://www.anarcocapitalista.com/textos/Lecciones%20de%20Economia%20con%20el%20Profesor%20Huerta%20de%20Soto%2028.pdf [Accessed 7 Mar 2021].

24. J. Huerta. Lecciones de economía lección 19 [no date] [Online] Available from: http://www.anarcocapitalista.com/textos/Lecciones%20de%20Economia%20con%20el%20Profesor%20Huerta%20de%20Soto%2019.pdf [Accessed 8 Mar 2021].

25. S. Ninpun. Keynes's Theory of Business Cycle. Economic Discussion [no date] [Online] Available from: https://www.economicsdiscussion.net/keynesian-economics/keynes-theory/keyness-theory-of-business-cycle-economics/26055 [Accessed 10 Mar 2021].

26. J. M. Keynes. The General Theory of Employment, Interest and Money. London: Macmillan, 1936, p.161.

27. J. Huerta. Money, Bank Credit and Economic Cycles. Auburn: Mises Institute, 1998, pp.542-565

28. J. Huerta. La teoría austriaca del ciclo económico. Cuadernos de Economía, 1980, 8.22, pp.257-272

29. C. N. Trueman. Hyperinflation and Weimar Germany. The History Learning Site, 2015 [Online] Available from: https://www.historylearningsite.co.uk/modern-world-history-1918-to-1980/weimar-germany/hyperinflation-and-weimar-germany/ [Accessed 11 Mar 2021].

30. K. Gilbert. The Story of Hyperinflation in Zimbabwe. World Atlas, 2017 [Online] Available from: https://www.worldatlas.com/articles/the-story-of-hyperinflation-in-zimbabwe.html [Accessed 11 Mar 2021].

31. Reserve Bank of Zimbabwe. Consumer Price Index 1979-2007 [Online] Available from: https://www.rbz.co.zw/index.php/research/markets/inflation [Accessed 11 Mar 2021].

32. R. Ndlovu. Zimbabwe Steps Closer to Hyperinflation With 737.3% Annual Rate. Bloomberg, 2020 [Online] Available from: https://www.bloomberg.com/news/articles/2020-07-14/zimbabwe-continues-its-march-back-to-hyperinflation [Accessed 11 Mar 2021].

33. Le Monde. Au Venezuela, l'inflation a été de 130 060 % en 2018. 2019 [Online] Available from: https://www.lemonde.fr/international/article/2019/05/29/venezuela-l-inflation-a-ete-de-130-060-en-2018_5469091_3210.html [Accessed 12 Mar 2021]

34. L. Cohen. IMF sees Venezuela inflation at 10 million percent in 2019. Reuters, 2018 [Online] Available from: https://www.reuters.com/article/venezuela-economy-idINKCN1MJ1YX?edition-redirect=in [Accessed 12 Mar 2021]

35. K. Down, M. Hutchinson & G. Kerr. The Coming Fiat Money Cataclysm and the Case for Gold. Cato Journal, 2012, Vol. 32, No. 2, pp.363-388

36. A. Volkov. How government's policies led to the Financial Crisis of 2008. A is A, 2017 [Online] Available from: https://medium.com/aisapodcast/how-governments-policies-led-to-the-financial-crisis-of-2008-4c060b6e5b7 [Accessed 13 Mar 2021]

37. P .Serhiy. The history of the creation and development of bitcoin. Cryptoobase, 2020 [Online] Available from: https://cryptoobase.com/the-history-of-the-creation-bitcoin/ [Accessed 15 Mar 2021]

38. S. Nakamoto. Bitcoin: A Peer-to-Peer Electronic Cash System. Bitcoin.org, 2009 [Online] Available from: https://bitcoin.org/bitcoin.pdf [Accessed 15 Mar 2021]

39. J. Frankenfield. Cryptocurrency. Investopedia, 2021 [Online] Available from: https://www.investopedia.com/terms/c/cryptocurrency.asp [Accessed 15 Mar 2021]

40. J. Lansky. Possible State Approaches to Cryptocurrencies. Journal of Systems Integration, 2018, Vol. 9, No. 1

41. L. Conway. Blockchain Explained. Investopedia, 2020 [Online] Available from: https://www.investopedia.com/terms/b/blockchain.asp [Accessed 15 Mar 2021]

42. J. Frankenfield. Proof of Work. Investopedia, 2021 [Online] Available from: https://www.investopedia.com/terms/p/proof-work.asp [Accessed 16 Mar 2021]

43. J. Frankenfield. Proof of Stake. Investopedia, 2019 [Online] Available from: https://www.investopedia.com/terms/p/proof-stake-pos.asp [Accessed 16 Mar 2021]

44. M. A. Russon. Crypto-currencies gaining popularity in Kenya. BBC News, 2019 [Online] Available from: https://www.bbc.com/news/business-47307575#:~:text=At%20the%20moment%2C%20the%20crypto-currencies%20Bitcoin%2C%20Dash%20and,small%20businesses%20to%20prove%20their%20creditworthiness%20for%20loans [Accessed 17 Mar 2021]

45. The Dogecoin Project. Dogecoin, 2021 [Online] Available from: https://dogecoin.com/ [Accessed 18 Mar 2021]

46. Bit Info Charts. Bitcoin Avg. Transaction Fee historical chart [Online] Available from: https://bitinfocharts.com/comparison/bitcoin-transactionfees.html [Accessed 18 Mar 2021]

47. Bit Info Charts. Dogecoin Avg. Transaction Fee historical chart [Online] Available from: https://bitinfocharts.com/comparison/dogecoin-transactionfees.html [Accessed 18 Mar 2021]

48. N. McCarthy. 1.7 Billion Adults Worldwide Do Not Have Access To A Bank Account. Forbes, 2017 [Online] Available from: https://www.forbes.com/sites/niallmccarthy/2018/06/08/1-7-billion-adults-worldwide-do-not-have-access-to-a-bank-account-infographic/?sh=507a67514b01 [Accessed 18 Mar 2021]

49. Z. Treu. Jamaican bobsled team raises $30,000 in Dogecoin for trip to Sochi. PBS, 2014 [Online] Available from: https://www.pbs.org/newshour/world/jamaican-bobsled-team-raises-30000-in-dogecoin-for-trip-to-sochi [Accessed 19 Mar 2021]

50. F. Saez. Apply the Cialdini's Principle of Consistency to Your Personal Productivity. FacileThings, 2017 [Online] Available from: https://facilethings.com/blog/en/cialdini-principle-of-consistency [Accessed 19 Mar 2021]

51. R. Preidt. Science Says: Smiling Helps You Get Happy. WebMD, 2019 [Online] Available from: https://www.webmd.com/mental-health/news/20190411/science-says-smiling-helps-you-get-happy [Accessed 19 Mar 2021]